Communication

Techniques For Assertive And Effective Communication, Figure Out How To Communicate Your Thoughts Clearly And Establish Clear Boundaries

(A No-nonsense Guide To Effective Communication For Couples)

Merle Warner

TABLE OF CONTENT

The Art Of Effective Communication For Managers 1

How To Make Better, More Powerful Exchanges Through The Use Of Empathy In Communication. An All-Purpose Guideline For Communication. 35

Recognizing The Steps In A Productive Communication Cycle 100

Consciousness Of Oneself 112

Communication And Models - Models Are Helpful In Communicating Since They Assist You Communicate 132

Pick Your Partner From The Box 148

The Art Of Effective Communication For Managers

In order for there to be successful communication in the workplace, both managers and employees need to be aware of how important it is. The ability of a manager to communicate clearly and effectively with the people under his or her supervision is critical to that management's success. When you stop and give it some thought, managing also involves communicating. Because the majority of a manager's responsibilities involve some type of communication, possessing strong communication abilities is absolutely necessary for that person to successfully carry out their work responsibilities. The following are some suggestions on managerial communication:

Capabilities in Verbal Communication

1. A Policy of Open Doors

When it comes to communication in the workplace, managers need to be as open and honest as they possibly can be in order to establish a culture of good communication. When this is done, there is an increased level of trust and comprehension throughout the organization.

It is imperative that workers are aware that they can speak with their management at any moment. In order to foster this feeling, supervisors should make it mandatory for all employees, regardless of their level of responsibility, to have access to open door policies. Listed below are some ideas that can help make your open door policy more successful:

a. Give your undivided attention to what is being spoken.

It is essential to your role as a manager that you have the ability to listen to and address the issues of your staff. It is up to you to ensure that they are not only heard but also get the impression that you are eager to provide a helpful hand.

b. Reschedule and continue with the original plan.

If you are currently in the middle of anything, it is courteous to ask your employee to come back at another time and reschedule the appointment. Be sure to get back to him or her as soon as you are able to after your schedule has cleared up.

c. Set a boundary for yourself

If an employee is abusing his privilege to come to your office, you should ask the department of human resources to resolve the situation. Or, if it is at all possible, try to solve the problem by yourself first. Describe the specific nature of the employee's infraction and offer some suggestions for how they could improve.

2. Always be Specific When Assigning Duties

When an employer clearly communicates their expectations to their workforce, they tend to produce higher levels of productivity. When delegating responsibilities, it is imperative that you remain specific and direct in your instructions.

You should attempt to avoid using terminology that the person you are trying to communicate with could find confusing, and you should replace complicated words with those that are easier to comprehend in order to make things more clear.

3. Reflect Before You Speak

Our feelings have the potential to get in the way of our decisions and actions, but as a manager, it is essential that you always appear cool and that you consider before you speak. Before making any sort of choice or taking any kind of action, you should think about all of the facts and go over the entire situation in order to improve your communication skills.

4. Keep an Open Mind Regarding Critique

It is essential for you, in the role of manager, to tackle any issues in a competent and professional manner. If people have criticisms about your management skills, you should think about whether or not the criticisms are valid and then work to improve.

5. Take Steps to Ensure That You Are Comprehended

It is the responsibility of a good manager to ensure that he is clear and that his staff understand him. You have a responsibility as a manager to oversee the process that your team follows, but you also have to make sure that your staff fully comprehend the tasks they are responsible for.

Instead of trying to manage groups, focus on managing individuals so that you can be sure your message is received. Because there is a lack of specificity inside groups, there may be a tendency for individuals to feel less accountable, which can lead to a free-rider problem in the workplace. When you are aiming to spread general information, use memos that address the majority; nevertheless, when it comes to giving out directions or individual comments, it is better if they are done face-to-face or in private. Memos that address the majority may be found here.

Participation from the audience

There is never only one-way communication between a speaker and their audience. But you, the speaker, are the one who has to make the first move in order for things to get going.

You may find that relaxing and feeling less isolated when you involve your audience in the process in some little way, which may also help them relax and feel less isolated. This may also be beneficial for you.

In the event that you are giving a humorous presentation or performing a stand-up comedy set about your experiences working in retail or catering, you might ask the audience to show of their hands in order to determine who else has had previous employment in these areas.

You may ask the audience a series of questions, then invite them to show you how knowledgeable they are by raising their hands and providing their best guesses.

Alternately, you might turn this situation on its head and devote some of your speaking time to fielding questions from the audience. This would be an interesting alternative.

It is crucial to have question-and-answer sessions because they provide the audience a chance to ask the speaker to elaborate on anything they have previously stated or to bring up a topic that they believe should have been discussed but has not been at this point in the presentation. This allows the speaker to demonstrate to the audience that their thoughts and viewpoints are respected, and that they are being listened to and that they are being attempted to have their point of view understood as a top priority.

In a similar vein, it may be quite effective to give the audience the opportunity to vote on anything that is connected to the talk or the evening as a whole as a whole (and it can occasionally be made amusing).

It's also possible for the speaker to recruit volunteers from the crowd to join them on stage (or some other analogous place) and assist with the demonstration.

Put your feelings on display for the world to see.

It is not necessarily to divulge insights about you that could be considered particularly personal, and which could cause discomfort or pain if they were to be revealed. In point of fact, this is not something that would likely be beneficial or appropriate.

This notion does not mean that you should tell your audience every single thing that is going on in your life or otherwise make them feel uncomfortable by informing them of things that they have no business knowing.

On the other hand, there have been occasions when I was delivering a presentation and, without intending to do so, realized that I was expressing my ideas in a manner in which I had not done so previously.

It is not about trying to come across as genuine, warm, and sincere; rather, it is about truly being genuine, warm, and sincere. When you wear your heart on your sleeve, you are demonstrating that you are genuine, warm, and sincere.

Naturally, if a speaker delivers stories or details that are manufactured, people of the audience may have a good reason to assume that this is the case, and as a result, they may feel alienated, or at the at least, less willing to listen to them or take them seriously.

Don't put too much stock in what you think of yourself.

Even if you are discussing serious topics, it is in your best interest as a public speaker to avoid getting too "heavy" and to keep your sense of humor at all times.

This will help the audience feel more at ease. That is not to mean that you should make jokes about the terrible things that are happening in the world or do anything else that is considered to be in poor taste.

However, it is essential that you do not alienate any members of the audience who might get disinterested in listening to the remainder of your presentation if you maintain an unyieldingly gloomy tone for the length of it.

Telling a tale about an embarrassing mistake you have made in the past can be a terrific icebreaker, provided that it is relevant to the aim and message of your lecture. Joking about who your celebrity lookalikes are can also be an effective way to break the ice.

In the same vein, it is essential to strike the appropriate balance and to avoid falling into the trap of being overly critical of one's own abilities.

The members of the audience do not wish to listen to a speaker who continuously criticizes themselves. Even if they are not the most outwardly confident speakers in general, the audience expects the speaker to have a certain degree of confidence in their self-worth and authority in speaking on the issue at hand. This is the case even if the speaker is not the most outwardly confident speaker. However, if they perfect the skill of playing down their experiences or their subject matter in a good-natured way from time to time, the audience may be less likely to feel alienated. This is because they will be able to see that they are not taking themselves too seriously.

Discuss issues that are relevant to the people in the audience.

Doing research on topics that the majority of the audience is likely to be familiar with is a fantastic idea, and they will thank you for it if it is at all possible.

You might draw on your experience and talk about specific elements of the location which your audience may be familiar with, particularly if they frequent it on a regular basis, if the event you are speaking at is somewhere you speak regularly or have spoken at in the past. If this is the case, you could draw on your expertise.

You should also steer clear of topics that could be considered offensive or which tend to spark a lot of debate. It's possible that some speakers will feel compelled to try to push the envelope with the topics they cover. Having said that, doing so can be perilous; so, my recommendation is that you err on the side of caution with regard to this matter. If it is impossible to avoid bringing up a controversial topic, the best course of action is to refrain from doing so in a manner that is opinion driven.

The Emperor gives you with the physical comforts of this world, but it is your responsibility to create. Children, a lovely home, and a successful career are all things that must be accomplished in order to gain success with the Emperor card. This must be done in conjunction with a twin flame, which is symbolized by the emperor card. As you travel through time with the Emperor, you will reflect on your life thus far and wonder what became of the person you once were.

Your accomplishments will make you feel pleased, but you will always have a part of you that wonders, despite all your success, if you have neglected the one thing that is the most important of all: the connection with your spirit. Because being in a relationship with your twin flame will eventually become too taxing for you, it is imperative that you maintain this connection while you are in a relationship with your twin flame. Because the twin flame with Emperor energy provides materialistic comfort, but expects you to provide emotional healing for both of them, you need to remain strong within yourself in order to survive. You are going to have to be the one to use discretion. You will need to take care of your twin flame in a loving manner. You will learn to be brave and courageous from the Emperor. After reuniting with your twin flame and engaging in a relationship with them, you will never be the same person again.

The Emperor is a metaphor for a relationship in which your twin flame is the more dominant partner and you are the one who needs to discover your own authentic, individual self. In the end, your roles will switch, and you will emerge as the most powerful of the bunch since you were able to learn from the very best (your twin flame, the energy of the Emperor).

TAROT OF THE ACE OF CUPS

When it comes to twin flame tarot readings, getting the Ace of Cups is generally a favorable omen to acquire, particularly if you are still in the beginning phases of the trip with your twin flame. If you see the Ace of Cups, it is a sign that you should have faith that the feelings you are experiencing are real and that you are moving in the correct way.

The first stages of twin flame love consist of the two people coming together and beginning a relationship. Let the relationship develop at its own pace and in its own time. Although it has the potential to flourish in the years to come, you shouldn't try to hasten events by placing an excessive amount of expectation on them at this key moment.

If you are already in a committed relationship with your twin flame, the Ace of Cups can sometimes portend the birth of a child, most often a female. This is the case if the card appears. As a result, the Ace is a good indication to look for if this is something that you hope to achieve.

Do you have a burning desire to find out how your twin flame really feels about you? Don't be concerned; the Ace indicates that they have nothing but genuine feelings for you. Your life's present manifestation of a twin flame is in the very early phases of falling in love.

Keep in mind, though, that your twin flame is not completely smitten with you just yet. Because this phase is still in its beginnings, you shouldn't place too much pressure on your twin flame just yet. Maintain a positive attitude and a carefree attitude; your twin flame will eventually accept your love and make it a priority in their own time.

Different Methods of Communicating

There are many methods of communication, but in this section, we will concentrate on the five most common ways that people communicate themselves. Even though we are all exposed to and make use of each of these approaches, not all of them are productive. When we make it a point to communicate in an authoritative manner, we get the finest results. Because the manner in which you express yourself will affect the kind of response you get, it is crucial to be conscious of the communication style you are utilizing in any circumstance. The same holds true for being able to comprehend the mode of communication that another individual employs. When we are able to recognize the ineffective communication style of another person, we are better able to combat that style and keep the dialogue on track.

1. Intensely combative

The other day, while I was getting groceries, I overheard some people using abusive language. When I was in line at the register, the woman in front of me started arguing with the cashier about a coupon. I got drawn into the argument. The item that she wanted to buy was not one that her coupon was valid for because it was for a different item. The woman started yelling and became irritated, and the cashier responded in kind by becoming more aggressive with the upset client. The scene rapidly deteriorated, and before long the woman was cursing and hurling items out of her suitcase as it became increasingly chaotic. The manager intervened, fetched the appropriate product for the coupon that was presented, and defused the tension in the situation. The woman's dishonest actions were ultimately rewarded, and she achieved the outcome that she had been working toward.

Whether it was being on the receiving end of a nasty email or engaging in a heated fight with a loved one, I'm confident that all of us have at some point or another experienced aggressive communication. But what exactly does it mean to communicate in an aggressive manner? And why does it usually make the conflict worse rather than finding a solution to it?

To put it more succinctly, any sort of communication that is designed to damage or control another person is considered to be aggressive communication. Aggression demonstrates a complete disregard for the other person and elevates the wants of the aggressor to the status of the only needs that are relevant or that merit discussion. Ignoring someone, yelling at them, calling them offensive names, or even threatening them or giving them an ultimatum are all examples of the numerous ways this behavior can manifest itself. Our natural response to violence is to become defensive, which can make the situation even worse because it adds gasoline to the fire. When someone is in a defensive position, they typically either give in to the aggressive conduct or confront it with what they consider to be enough force to convince the other person to back off. However, a skilled communicator will have the ability, as well as the emotional control necessary, to bring the situation back under control. He will interpret the aggressive behavior as a sign of weakness, have the ability to master his emotional reaction to the behavior, and ultimately come out on top.

Aggression may provide results, but it is never a fruitful method to achieve a solution; rather, it typically culminates in a standoff or even a violent conflict. Aggression may produce results, but it is never a productive approach to reach a solution. When communicated in an aggressive manner, one risks appearing confrontational, unpleasant, and condescending. It is essential that you are conscious of how you come across to other people and that you make it a point to ensure that the manner in which you communicate fosters an atmosphere in which fruitful conversation can flourish.

In the preceding illustration, the belligerent behavior of the client demonstrated a lack of respect for the cashier and a failure on her part to inform herself before to making her statement. Even if she was incorrect, she did not believe that it made a difference. The cashier took exception at the disrespect shown to her by the angry client and retaliated in kind with aggressive behavior, which only served to stoke the fires of the conflict. After conducting an analysis of the scenario, determining what the issue was, and suggesting a remedy, the issue was eventually resolved. In this circumstance, there was no reaching of a compromise, and nobody gave up anything of value. If the communication approach had been different, the outcome would not have changed; but, the problem would have been solved considerably more rapidly and in a manner that was significantly more favorable.

2. Involved in deception

The act of transmitting communications with the intention of influencing or controlling the conduct of another person is an example of manipulative communication. While it has the potential to be utilized to accomplish beneficial results, it also has the potential to be used to control and manipulate other people. A prime illustration of deceptive communication can be seen in the film "The Godfather." One of the most memorable scenes in the film depicts Michael Corleone attempting to persuade his brother-in-law Carlo Rizzi to take the rich offer that the Corleone family has to offer. He achieves this goal by preying on Carlo's emotions and anxieties, leading Carlo to believe that he is trapped and has no other options. Although Carlo is made to believe that Michael's offer is an incredible opportunity that he simply cannot pass up, it is widely understood that the offer really means that Carlo will be murdered if he does not comply with the conditions. Although this is an extreme example, it displays rather clearly how manipulative communication can be used to control and influence other people.

Communicators who manipulate their audience by playing on their feelings in order to forward their own agenda frequently resort to the use of deceitful language. They could flatter someone or try to exploit their fears in order to convince that person to accomplish what they want. They might also lie to themselves or hide information in order to keep control of the circumstance. Even though manipulative communication can be successful in the short term, in the long term it will almost always result in the destruction of relationships. Manipulative communicators will eventually be exposed, which will gain them a reputation for being untrustworthy and will make it harder for them to form relationships that will last.

This mode of communication is an art, and it can be challenging to determine whether there is an element of manipulation at play. There are a number of telltale symptoms of manipulative communication, including the use of guilt trips, being pressured into a decision, ignoring someone on purpose, and playing on a person's anxieties. When we are unable to express our demands and requirements in a straightforward manner, we put ourselves in danger of adopting a communication style that is manipulative. Although it may feel more natural to utilize a manipulative strategy even when one does not want to cause harm, it is always preferable to communicate in an open and honest manner.

3. Self-assured

A person's communication style can be described as assertive if they are able to respect the rights and beliefs of others while at the same time standing up for their own rights and opinions. Individuals who are assertive are able to plainly and immediately convey their opinions and feelings without resorting to either aggression or passivity. They are also skilled at negotiating solutions to disagreements that benefit both parties.

Take, for instance, the scenario in which you have been tasked with completing a project at work but you believe that you either lack the necessary time or the necessary skills to do so. It's possible that a passive person will agree to participate in the project, but then they'll either try to find out how to do it on their own or they'll just do a job that's just half-hearted and hope that no one sees. A person who is aggressive may inform their supervisor that they are not going to perform the project, or they may execute the project, but they may purposefully do a lousy job of it. A self-assured person would tell their manager the truth about the problem, express their concerns, and then make a request for assistance or greater resources. This method, which takes a more proactive stance, has a greater chance of resulting in a beneficial end for both parties involved.

You can have the habit of confusing forceful speech with aggressive communication; many people make this mistake. On the other hand, the contrast between the two is striking. A healthy kind of communication is called assertiveness, and it entails expressing one's opinions and feelings in a manner that is straightforward, courteous, and honest. Communicators that are assertive are crystal clear on the genuine wants they have for themselves and have the self-assurance to ask for what they require. They do not interrupt people and pay close attention to what is being said even if they disagree with what is being said.

Being assertive does not mean acting in a demanding or domineering manner. Finding a happy medium between advocating for oneself and listening to others, with the understanding that the priorities of each group should be given equal weight, is the goal here. In every kind of relationship, the most effective method to express who you are and what you want is to use assertive communication. Being assertive in your personal relationships can assist you in establishing boundaries, communicating your needs and desires, and finding constructive ways to resolve conflict. Being assertive in professional settings can aid in the development of solid working relationships, the demonstration of one's value, the conduct of fruitful negotiations, and the management of challenging talks. In relationships that are based on transactions, assertive communication is communication that gets straight to the point, demonstrates respect for the other person, and commands respect from that person in return.

4. Non-active

A person engages in passive communication when they do not communicate their own wants, needs, or opinions during a conversation. Passive communication is a type of communication. They, on the other hand, provide others the ability to influence the situation. This is something that can occur in verbal as well as nonverbal communication. A passive communicator may, for instance, avoid making eye contact, employ language that is ambiguous, or defer to the opinions of others while making judgments. Even while there are times and situations in which passive communication is appropriate, employing it too frequently can bring about unintended consequences. Individuals who are passive communicators may have difficulties standing up for themselves, which can lead to them being exploited by others because of their inability to speak up for themselves.

Individuals, however, can learn to employ passive communication in a manner that is more beneficial for them if they have an understanding of how to recognize and control passive communication. When talking with other people, it is essential to give careful consideration to the words you choose to employ. Try to steer clear of words such as "I don't know" or "whatever you want to do is fine with me." Not only do statements like these give the impression that you do not have an opinion of your own, but they also give the impression that you are uninterested in the dialogue that is taking place. The same can be said for the practice of questioning. Asking questions may give the impression of weakness, which is not the case, contrary to the beliefs of many people who engage in passive communication. When you show a desire to thoroughly comprehend anything by asking clarifying questions, the other person will have faith that you are invested in the topic since you are showing that you want to fully understand it.

Because it might be interpreted as a sort of avoidance or a lack of interest in the topic being discussed, passive communication can make it challenging to develop meaningful connections with other people. People who engage in passive communication typically make the assumption that others already know what they are thinking or working for, and they leave the responsibility for better understanding them on the shoulders of the other person. If you ever have the impression that your significant other, your boss, a friend, or a member of your family does not appreciate some of your best attributes, it is important to review how you communicate with those people. Do people perceive you to have those qualities?

5. submission-based

Communication that is submissive seeks to avoid controversy at all costs. It entails articulating goals and requirements in a manner that is neither intimidating nor confrontational to the other person. For instance, a submissive communicator would ask, "Do you want to help me with the dishes, or should I do them on my own?" rather than stating, "I need you to do the dishes." This is because a submissive communicator avoids asserting their needs. In exceptional circumstances, this strategy may prove useful; nonetheless, there is almost always a superior, more forceful alternative that may be taken. A submissive communicator, for instance, may be less inclined to speak up in meetings or confront a coworker about a problem in a setting such as a workplace, where they may be less likely to speak up in meetings.

There are drawbacks associated with continuously using a subservient voice, despite the fact that this strategy can be helpful if the primary objective is to avoid disagreement and move on. People who communicate in a submissive manner could have trouble standing up for themselves, and their requirements might not be properly understood or realized. When you speak in a submissive manner, you are sending the message to others that you consider your thoughts or contributions to be beneath them.

How To Make Better, More Powerful Exchanges Through The Use Of Empathy In Communication. An All-Purpose Guideline For Communication.

Have you ever received a compliment on your ability to communicate verbally?

When you say something, do they find that it has an impact on them? Or do you utilize a notion in order to generate an image that is meaningful for your audience to comprehend?

In exchange, they may improve your ability to communicate verbally.

Here's what I think is happening:
You have a strong vocabulary with a wide variety of words to choose from.

You have a Sensitive Heart.

Permit me to clarify by breaking this down into four sections, which will cover what empathy is, how it works when interacting with other people, specific instances in which to practice empathic communication, and a concluding comment on leadership. I will begin by defining empathy and then moving on to how it functions when talking with other people.

Whether you are a creator, a business leader, an entrepreneur, a writer, a public speaker, a social media influencer, a teacher, a parent, a spouse, a friend, a relative, a neighbor, or pretty much anything else that has anything to do with being a human, you may want to keep this idea in mind as the catalyst for all future forms of communication.

An Effective Definition of Empathy in Communication.

How exactly can you improve your communication skills through the application of empathy?

Naturally, you most likely already let empathy influence the manner that you speak. We are always being influenced by other people, regardless of whether or not we are aware of this fact. This has an effect on the things that we say as well as the method that we say them.

George Herbert Mead is incorrect when he asserts that you live on an island. Any individual is continually impacted by and lives following what the social sphere has delivered them, or what he refers to as "A Social Self." Therefore, it might be crucial to simply be aware of how you are connected to others and to be deliberate about how you choose to allow that to influence your communication. You have already been influenced by the actions of other people.

The next opportunity is to purposefully take action while keeping those aspects in mind and deciding between specific options while keeping the perspectives of other individuals in mind.

Consider a scenario in which you awaken and dress, which is likely something you anticipated because it is traditional in our culture to wear clothing and something you have been influenced by (which, even the opinion not to wear clothes is often done out of a conscious or deliberately rebellious act against said influence). There is a good chance that even the ground in your bedroom or in your closet is covered in garments. And not just any clothes, as the type of clothing is presumably specific to the cultural standards of your society; out of all the choices for clothing that are out there in the world, we frequently just consider a chosen handful of them. It makes little difference what you chose to put inside or on your body because it has already been shaped by the choices of other individuals.

However, rather than simply donning whatever you feel like wearing (one again, likely influenced by the social sphere), you may also want to think about who you're going to meet or what sort of situation you'll be in, as well as what kinds of clothing options will best complement your intended presence in those contexts. This can help you decide what to wear.

You would not only need to be knowledgeable with the norms and influences of society in order to successfully prosecute, but you would also need to take into consideration the viewpoints of the individuals involved and what your choices in dress will convey to them. In order to successfully prosecute, you would not only need to be familiar with the norms and influences of society, but you would also need to dress professionally. I take it that you want them to have a professional impression of you, is that correct? You have the choice of wearing in a way that the other people involved will find appealing and that the culture as a whole thinks to be appropriate for a professional setting (empathy).

Do you feel like breaking with convention and dressed more casually than everyone else for the meeting by donning a hoodie and a hat? Since you are functioning inside a norm (influence) (empathy), you are choosing to send a message that is counter-cultural based on how you expect the other people involved will interpret your casual clothes in light of those standards. This choice is based on how you believe the other people will react to the fact that you are breaking those standards.

Even though we have only covered clothing, we have still been able to cover a substantial percentage of everything else despite the fact that we have only covered one topic.

In spite of the fact that our social reality is the way that it is, egocentrism appears to be ingrained in people. Because of this, employing empathy is a means to force oneself to work against one's natural impulses. Your transition away from being passively influenced by the activities of other people and toward actively drawing on and profiting from the influence of others. Because your actions will already have an effect on you, demonstrating empathy for others demands you to make decisions with an increased level of forethought, purpose, and calculation.

Then, How Can Empathy Function Within Our Varied Circumstances?

Empathy is the capacity to take on the perspective of another person and to think, feel, and behave as if one were in that person's position. Empathy makes better communication possible.

You may change your communication to what will be most useful for the transaction since you are always communicating to someone else. This is made possible when you inhabit their mind and observe the world from their perspective (an empathetic process known as, you guessed it, "Perspective Taking"). You are able to make conscious decisions if you look further than the default influence and use the literal point of view of the other person as your guidance.

The next issue that needs to be answered is, "How exactly will doing so improve our communication?"

A valid question to ask

It is important to keep in mind that conveying empathy and adjusting your behavior to fit the circumstances do not require you to tell other people whatever it is they wish to hear. When trying to steer someone in a new direction for their future, it is sometimes necessary to be aware of where they currently are.

This may cause others to comment that you have a natural talent for communicating through language.

Considering that you are, in fact, engaging in this activity.

You are quite good at modifying the way you speak in accordance with the people who are listening to you.

2. There Is More to Communication Than Just the Exchange of Words, Paraphrase

It is imperative that we never forget that communication entails much more than merely the words that are spoken between parties; rather, it encompasses everything that is utilized in the process of passing on a message or piece of information to a receiver. In order to accomplish this, you will need to put yourself in the position of your audience and make the necessary adjustments.

In light of this, empathic communication requires more than simply adapting one's message to the specific information that one's target audience requires hearing. Furthermore, it requires the following:

due to the fact that it is essential for them to listen to it,

to the people who have a requirement to do so or who absolutely must hear it,

the method in which they are required to listen to it,

as well as the driving force behind their initial interest in having it conveyed to them.

You are required to ask all of these questions, and you must be prepared to settle for the response that is written the best.

When delivering a message, empathic communication involves taking into account all of the different possible consequences, rather than only changing your wording.

For instance, I am going to make the assumption that you would like to see this mapped out in more detail (a table would be ideal; if only I weren't so lazy...

In light of the fact that my attempts at empathic contact with you have been unsuccessful, please allow me to make an effort to change what it is that I intend to say in order to cater to your preferences.

If communication involves more than just the exchange of words, you need to take the following into consideration:

Which terms are you going to employ, taking into account the recipient's vocabulary as well as their level of comprehension?

How those words ought to be put together, including the positioning of information and the significance of that positioning to the overarching message, the utilization of illustrations or narratives, the tone and style, as well as any other non-verbals that complement your words, as well as the timing and positioning of particular phrases.

what the length needs to be, which suggests that there will be times when you are unable to explain everything that you would like to say.

Which medium do you choose to communicate on; while this question is mostly pertinent to interpersonal (relationship-based) communication, it is equally relevant to any material you may be creating.

Which of the following best describes the context of the message: the apparent authority, trustworthiness, or voice of the sender? It's possible that you'll need to adjust your context so that you can get along with the other person as well as possible. It may be necessary to subvert a predefined framework in order to strengthen your message (for instance, a parent renouncing their authority in order to empower their child; this type of communication is known as "Complementary Communication" with regard to authority).

How should the message fit with the surrounding environment, both physically and geographically? This comprises the location of the recipient, the time it was delivered, the recipient's mental and emotional states, and the time it was delivered.

Because of this, others could start to comment that you have a natural talent for words.

Considering that you are acting in this manner.

You are quite good at modifying the way you speak in accordance with the people who are listening to you.
2. There Is More to Communication Than Just Words, Paraphrase

It is imperative that we never forget that communication encompasses much more than merely the words that are spoken; rather, it is comprised of anything and everything that delivers a message or information to a receiver. To accomplish this, you must place yourself in the position of your audience and make the necessary adjustments.

Because of this, empathic communication entails more than merely adapting your message to fit the requirements of your audience in order to be effective. Additionally, It Involves

the importance of them being able to listen to it,

to the people who have a requirement to do so or who really must,

the tone with which it must be conveyed to them,

and the motivation that drove them to want to hear it in the first place.

You are required to make all of these inquiries, and you must be prepared to accept the response that is written the finest.

When you communicate a message, empathic communication means taking into account all of the possible outcomes; it is not merely modifying your words.

For example, I am going to make the assumption that you would like to see this mapped out in more detail (a table would be ideal; if only I weren't so lazy...

Allow me to make an effort to change what I want to say in order to cater to your preferences in light of the fact that the previous attempt at empathic contact with you was unsuccessful.

If communication entails more than just the exchange of words, you need to take into consideration the following:

Which terms are you going to employ, taking into account the recipient's vocabulary and level of comprehension?

How those words ought to be put together, including the positioning of information and the significance of that positioning to the overarching message, the utilization of illustrations or narratives, the tone and style, as well as any other non-verbals that complement your words, as well as the timing and positioning of certain phrases.

what the length has to be, which suggests that there will be times when you are unable to explain everything you would like to say.

the media do you choose to communicate on; this is primarily pertinent to interpersonal (relationship-based) communication, but it also pertains to any material you may be creating. This question is about the medium you prefer to communicate on.

What is the sender's context, including their apparent authority, trustworthiness, and voice in relation to the message? It's possible that you'll need to adjust your context in order to make the other person feel most comfortable. It may be necessary to subvert a predefined framework in order to strengthen your message (for instance, a parent renouncing their authority in order to empower their child; this type of communication is referred to as "Complementary Communication" with regard to authority).

In what kind of a physical or geographical setting should the message be delivered? This comprises the location of the recipient, the time it was delivered, the recipient's mental and emotional states, and the time it was delivered.

This type of communication, which goes beyond only utilizing words to convey meaning, is referred to as "Non-Verbal Communication." You have a responsibility as a parent to be conscious of your nonverbal cues, such as closeness, touch, facial expressions, location, and other nonverbal cues that are associated with whatever it is that you are saying. Even when you are not directly communicating with your children, you still need to be aware of the messages that you are sending them.

If communication involves more than just words, then everything you do is a form of communication, and it is essential that you transmit the messages you are trying to convey in an empathic manner.

The Leader Is Not an Exception to This;

When you give a speech, preside over a meeting, or send out an email, you are required to demonstrate more than just sympathy for your audience. Everything you do and participate in, from the space you create to the way you move in relation to the people around you, how you hold yourself, and the activities you do, all tell something about you.

Because of this, a corporation may use flowery language in its advertisements or the postings it makes on social media, but they may still cause substantial problems if they violate an ethical ideal that is important to the consumers they are trying to attract.

If Marshall McLuhan was right when he said that the medium is the message, then we will want all of our channels to deliver our messages in an empathic manner.

3. The Specifics Are Extremely Important

Let's begin by recognizing that not every statement or act of communication will be heard or understood by the people in your audience. You probably did not commit every word of this chapter to memory, and it's possible that you didn't even read it all very attentively.

As a consequence of this, there is no need for you to worry about each individual word, right?

In fact, I'd argue that the opposite is the case. It is imperative that every phrase, every decision made within the composition, and every component be intentional. Poets may be the most effective communicators because they are required to work within precise restrictions, which elevate the significance of each word they employ. Your audience will be able to follow the flow of your presentation even if they are not paying attention to each individual word because each word has been carefully selected.

Due to bad writing, inefficient language, or distracting substance, an audience will deem the messenger to be inexperienced, and as a result, they will make the conscious decision that the message is not worthy of their attention. Even texts with a pleasant tone will be ignored.

However, even if they aren't entirely digested, strong verbal and nonverbal cues can help people become more open and empowered to accept the messages they need to hear. This is true even if the cues themselves aren't fully absorbed. When you tell a tale, there are times when you include details that aren't the main point because they help the audience absorb the main idea even if they don't recall the details afterward. In the same way, there are times when you add details that aren't the main point when you explain something.

Even though the audience may not appreciate each detail to the same degree as you do and even though it may not feel like it is worth your time, paying attention to every element will build a flow that will decide how the audience judges to embrace whatever it is that you are doing. This is true even though it is possible that they may not enjoy each detail to the same degree that you do.

Therefore, design your work with the delicacy of a poet and carry each detail with the care and attention it deserves.

4. The Benefits of Having Self-Empathy

Being empathetic with other people may give the impression that it is required to put one's own needs on the back burner during interactions with other people and instead cater to the interests of the other party in order to achieve one's own goals or fulfill another's needs.

It is not the case.
We are obligated to acknowledge that internalizing such presumption has the potential to be highly detrimental for some personalities:

though you have a personality that is driven by your ego, you will lie about who you are in order to get what you want from other people and will regularly adopt several identities in order to make it appear as though other people want you to do certain things.

If you have a "helping" disposition, you will prioritize the happiness of others before your own needs and wants.

If you have a mindset that is people-pleasing or conciliatory, you will avoid awkward interactions in an effort to keep the peace and calm that you have created for others.

Sometimes the process of empathizing will inform you that in order to reveal unhealthy behaviors and push people toward health, you need to create a message that isn't completely what your audience wants to hear. This is necessary in order to expose unhealthy behaviors and urge people toward health. If you totally reject or forget what it is that you offer to the conversation, you will lose both yourself and the value that you bring to the process.

If you want to put it another way, perhaps a better way to say it is that you can only adopt the perspective of another person when you have fully owned your own.

It is impossible to have genuine empathy for another person without first having it for oneself.

If you don't know who you are, what you need, what you have to offer, the vocabulary you've gathered, or the content of what you bring to the table, your communication will always be a vacuous attempt to please you and will be less successful as a result.

You can't let empathy make you forget who you are; rather, it should motivate you to be the most convincing version of yourself in the communications you generate. Whether you are a leader or in a relationship, whatever you say must correctly represent who you are on the inside, while also adapting to the circumstances of the other person. This is true whether you are in a relationship or a leadership position.

This is what people mean when they talk about being self-aware or "knowing oneself." After that, you will finally be able to make accommodations that are suitable, healthy, and attributed to your audience.
It is important to keep in mind that you, too, are a member of the audience, just like the poet.

Even if great content can be produced with less effort, you still need to give serious consideration to every word you write since you will ultimately be held accountable for what you produce.

You have to go through the process of self-empathy because you understand that you will benefit from anything you create, even if it is meant to be given to another person.

As you compose a message, you will make adjustments to it...

Never forget to keep that in mind.

Each and every one of us engages in the daily activity of listening. The idea that we should all be competent in it is one that is founded on acceptable grounds. Sadly, the majority of us have terrible listening skills. Only around half of what is said in any one discussion can be remembered by the typical person. This falls even further to 25% throughout the next 48 hours. It effectively indicates that we are only able to remember approximately one quarter of the information that is really presented to us. A sizeable portion of the general population suffers from a deficiency in their listening abilities. Because of this, mistakes are made, opportunities are lost, communication breaks down, and misunderstandings lead to broken relationships. You will be able to change all of this, though, after you understand how to become an active listener. Now is the moment to come to terms with the fact that talking is only one aspect of a conversation. Instead, there must also be somebody who is listening to what is being said. If that weren't the case, wouldn't all of us end up yelling over one another? You are going to discover how to become an active listener as well as the many styles of listening, the frequent obstacles to active listening, and how to get beyond those obstacles in this chapter.

Different kinds of listening

There is, contrary to what you may have been led to believe, more than one way to listen to something. Listening can be broken down into two categories: active and passive.

As its name suggests, the act of hearing something or someone without giving that item or person your whole attention is referred to as passive listening. When the person who is speaking receives little to no feedback, or none at all, the communication is typically unidirectional. The listener's ability to hear the speaker is severely hindered in this setting. It does not need any effort on the part of the listener, but in most cases, the passive listener winds up losing out on significant aspects of the conversation since they were not paying attention to it. Have you ever made a passing gesture toward someone, such as nodding your head or maintaining eye contact, even though you were not paying attention to what they were saying? There is a good chance that you were daydreaming or thinking about anything else at the time. If you answered yes, then you were not an active listener.

On the other hand, "active listening," which is exactly what it sounds like, is when a person pays attention to what is being said while doing so. The attention of the listener is completely drawn to the content of what is being communicated as a result of this. These types of listeners typically provide feedback either occasionally or after the speaker has completed their statement. If you give everything you have to what is being said to you, you will have a far better chance of understanding and retaining the knowledge that is being given with you. It lessens the likelihood of misconceptions and miscommunications occurring as a result. In addition to all of this, it guarantees that you have a complete comprehension of what is being said.

Poor Techniques in terms of Listening

A variety of distractions inhibit attentive listening. The details are as described below.

Listening Only Partially

The vast majority of us just listen in part. Have you ever been engaged in a conversation with a person over the phone while also focusing on something else? It's possible that while someone else was talking to you, you were multitasking by looking through the pages of a magazine, checking your email, or even browsing through your social media feeds. You were not paying attention to what was being spoken to you in that particular occasion. Instead, you were busy with other things. If you are engaging in any kind of multitasking when another person is speaking to you, then you are only partially listening to what they are saying.

Opinions or Prejudices

There are times when the listener might have certain preconceived notions about the person who is speaking. Or, it's possible that they have already formed an opinion on them before they have even spoken a word. Because of these preconceived notions and snap judgments, you are unable to comprehend the whole meaning of what the other person is saying. It's possible that you've formed an opinion about them based on the way they dress, the way they act, or even the way they carry themselves. This idea that you already have in your head will cloud everything else that they say, preventing you from fully and genuinely comprehending what is being communicated to you.

Anything Unfavorable

Your ability to completely comprehend what is being communicated will be hindered, just as it will be if you have any preconceived notions or judgments about the person doing the communicating. This is due to the fact that you have previously established that you do not agree with the speaker or their opinions. Because of this, there is always some degree of distortion in the message that is being delivered, which raises the likelihood that it will be misunderstood as well as misread. It's possible, for instance, that you and the person speaking to you hold very different ideas. This will be in direct opposition to everything that you hold dear. Because of this, there is a good probability that you will find that you are unable to agree with what is being said. In a similar vein, there is a good likelihood that you are not paying the person who is speaking to you your entire attention.

Lacking in Confidence

A lack of self-assurance can also prevent one from actively listening to what others have to say. If you already have a strong thought about yourself that you will not understand what is being stated to you, your willingness to really listen will decrease as a result of this notion. After all, if you have already concluded that you will not be successful, there is no use in making an effort.

Lack of Capacity for Tolerance

There are times when certain individuals are unable to listen to what the others have to say because they are highly thrilled to give their thoughts or have questions that they want to have answered. No matter what it is, if you interrupt the other person on a regular basis, you will not be able to comprehend what it is that they are saying in its whole. This is one of the many reasons why you are expected to participate in the conversation with your whole attention at all times and to just listen when other people are talking. If you continually cut off the person who is speaking, you will never be able to comprehend what it is that they are attempting to convey.

The Value of Being an Active Listener

It is never too late to improve your listening skills if you are not already a good listener. Your motivation to make this change can be increased, just like it can be increased for any other aspect of your life, by understanding a little bit about the rewards that you can get. In this section, let's have a look at all the various advantages that come along with practicing active listening.

Information Recall Your capacity to remember and recall specific information improves when you pay attention to the person speaking to you and actively listen to them. If you are preoccupied with something else, you will not be able to give your complete attention to the activities going on around you. Because of this, you are unable to pay attention to what is being stated. For instance, if the speaker is providing advise or directions on how to complete a specific work and you zone out throughout the conversation, you won't be aware of what needs to be completed. Always give your whole attention to the person who is speaking to you so that you can avoid getting caught in precarious circumstances like these.

Find Solutions to Issues

When you pay attention to what other people have to say, it will help you become better at finding solutions to problems. It is helpful in identifying any challenges or problems that others are going through. Because of this, you will be able to assist them in fixing their problems. You will become more conscious of the issues even if you do nothing more than listen to the information that is being communicated to you. The sooner the issue is identified, the sooner it may be fixed once it's been identified.

Developing Relationships and Links

When you give someone your undivided attention and focus when they are speaking to you, it inherently inspires them to talk back to you. If someone listened to what you had to say with patience, do you think it would make you more likely to listen to what they had to say? Extending this civility to other people helps strengthen the relationships you have with them. Additionally, it encourages constructive conversation. Your capacity for empathy toward other people will increase along with your willingness to listen to what they have to say and your capacity to comprehend what they are saying. This one easy gesture can go a long way toward increasing the quality of your interactions with others. Additionally, it makes interacting with other people less difficult.

Enhance Your Prior Understanding

Learning is impossible unless you actively pay attention to what other people have to say and share. For example, you are attending a business seminar where you are being instructed on useful business procedures, but you choose not to pay attention because you do not like the person who is giving the presentation. It's possible that you've been left in the dark about crucial information that could have been beneficial to you and your company. If you had only been listening, you could have avoided all of this trouble. When you take the time to pay attention to what people around you are saying and actively listen to what they have to say, you can gain useful insights into a variety of facets of life. Keep in mind that no two people are exactly the same and that as a result, we all have different ways of thinking, acting, and behaving. You can expand your knowledge by watching how other people behave and by paying attention to what they have to say.

Establishing Credibility

When one person listens to another person talk without interjecting or disrupting, it is much simpler to develop trust in a connection between the two people. If you keep interrupting the person who is attempting to communicate something to you, they will become disinterested in the conversation you are having with them. Even if they want to talk to you about something in the future, it's possible that they won't even approach you. It is imperative that you give full attention to what is being said to you in order to prevent the occurrence of the aforementioned scenario. They will feel more at ease talking to you if you learn how to listen without interrupting the speaker once you have mastered this skill. This serves to strengthen the relationships between us, and it also helps to boost the level of trust we have in each other. This benefit is useful at all levels, regardless of whether the connection in question is professional or personal.

Keeping Misunderstandings at a Minimum

The fact that most of us just listen in order to formulate a response is one of the most prominent factors contributing to misunderstandings. We are not listening with the intent to comprehend. Instead, we are making mental calculations and coming up with plans for our reactions. Relationships are prone to developing conflicts, fights, and misunderstandings as a result of this factor. When these factors are not controlled, they have the potential to quickly destroy even the healthiest of relationships. Listening attentively to what is being said is the quickest and easiest way to prevent misunderstandings and errors in communication. If you have any questions or concerns that you believe require clarification, you can always ask the speaker after they have completed expressing their thoughts and ideas. Instead than assuming the worst and misinterpreting what was said, wouldn't this method be more productive and less stressful in its attempt to fix the problem?

How to Develop Into a Person Who Listens Actively

Developing into an active listener and honing your listening abilities is something that will benefit all of the connections you have throughout your life. Some people have an innate ability to listen well, while others have to put in the effort to improve their listening skills. You may improve your ability to actively listen with some deliberate practice and time spent doing so. The following are some pointers that will prove useful at various points along the way.

Absolutely No Distractions

The first and most important guideline of active listening is to eliminate any potential sources of distraction. However, focusing on external distractions is not the only thing that needs to be done. You must also get rid of the distractions that are coming from within yourself. Let's put our attention for the time being on exterior distractions because it is relatively simple to cope with them. When you are chatting to someone, you should refrain from looking at your phone, reading, replying to emails, or engaging in any other activity that could be perceived as a distraction from the conversation. You should do everything that is required to guarantee that you get rid of these extractions as soon as possible. Instead, you should only concentrate on what is actually being spoken.

It takes more work to be able to avoid distractions from within. If you are not accustomed to being a good listener, there is a strong chance that you are easily distracted by the various things that are going through your head at any given moment. It is time to put these ideas to rest and direct all of your attention to the conversation at hand. If you feel as though you are losing attention, consciously bring it back to the information that is being communicated with you. Making progress in this area requires hard work and consistent practice. When you finally figure out how to quiet the chatter in your head, you'll have a far better chance of completely comprehending what other people are saying. Additionally, it heightens your awareness and mindfulness.

Both the Content and the Context Are Important

It is of the utmost significance that you pay close attention to the words that the other person is saying. You shouldn't only focus on the meaning of the words themselves; instead, you should pay attention to the situation in which they are being spoken. When placed in a certain setting, certain concepts and expressions might communicate a meaning that is distinct from their original intent. Hearing what the other person has to say will assist in comprehending what it is they are talking about. Nevertheless, if you pay attention to the context, you'll be able to pick up on any recurring themes as well as any underlying tones that aren't being openly communicated. It is imperative that you give their words and the ideas they have expressed in a certain setting your undivided attention.

It's All About How You Carry Yourself

When you are listening to someone, you should always be aware of how your body language conveys what you are hearing. Body language is important not just when you are the one doing the talking, but also when you are the one doing the listening. The message that you are either paying attention to what is being said or are disinterested in what is being said can be conveyed by your body language, which is an extremely effective communication tool. You are going to need to project body language that suggests that you are actively listening to the conversation and that you are involved in it. Making sure that your torso is facing the person who is speaking to you and that you are bending toward them to some degree is the easiest method to accomplish this task. Do not lean forward to the point where you are invading their personal space, as this is considered rude. Do you remember how, in the last chapter on body language, you were given an introduction to various approaches that would help you project the ideal body language? Now is the time to start putting it all to use, so get to it! When someone is speaking to you, it is helpful to behave in a manner that is similar to the speaker so that they feel more at ease.

In terms of body language, you need to make sure that you are maintaining an appropriate amount of eye contact while avoiding gazing at the person who is speaking. It's a bit much if you find yourself staring at the speaker without blinking for long periods of time. It may give the impression of hostility. When they are speaking, it is important that you keep a level of eye contact that is comfortable for you. The speaker will lose interest in you if you do not maintain an eye contact level that is comfortable for them or if you refuse to make eye contact.

Take Note of Your Feelings

Be sure to pay attention to the speaker's feelings as well as their words when they are talking to you. You will not be successful at this endeavor unless you are actively participating in the discussion. If you pay attention to the underlying feelings or the undercurrent, you can glean a great deal of additional information about what is being said. Additionally, it permits you to obtain a better understanding of the perspective of the person speaking to you. This makes it simpler to interact with other people. The vast majority of us are unable to transmit information in a robotic manner. Typically, our feelings are what lead us in the right direction. Taking note of their feelings will help you determine the appropriate course of action to take in response to what they have said. For instance, smiling at someone who appears to be sad is not the best idea in the world. On the other hand, if they are talking about something interesting, your grin can be a boost to their confidence. This helps to keep the dialogue going in a healthy way.

Promote the use of verbal cues.

It is possible to provoke a reaction or response from the speaker by making use of verbal cues, which are of great use in this regard. An occasional "yes," "I understand," or simply "hmm" while another person is speaking demonstrates that you are paying attention to what they are saying. You can also convey the same meaning through the use of additional gestures, such as giving an occasional nod or smiling.

In addition to making use of verbal signals, you should also pay close attention to any verbal cues that are provided to you by the speaker. It's possible that they downplay a certain aspect of the argument or emphasize particular terms. When they are talking about something, they could even employ a different tone of voice or pause in between statements. The speaker clearly wants you to pay close attention to everything that they are saying, as evidenced by all of these cues. If there is quiet, it is possible that they are waiting for a reaction from you; in these situations, demonstrating that you have understood what they have said is sufficient to satisfy their expectation of a response from you. You should go on to the following recommendation if you haven't fully absorbed what they are stating to you.

Helps When You Paraphrase

In addition to encouraging the speaker to provide vocal clues, one of the best ways to demonstrate that you are listening is to paraphrase the information that is being communicated by the speaker. Restating information in your own words demonstrates to the other person that you were paying attention to what they said. Additionally, it permits the person who is speaking to know that you have understood what they are saying to you completely. It gives you the opportunity to get things clarified if you have any questions or feel as though you haven't fully comprehended something. Clarifying what another person has said in a casual chat is a great way to offer support as well as understanding for that person. When you paraphrase material in a professional context, you demonstrate that you have obtained an accurate understanding of what was presented to you.

Questions With No Right Answers

The practice of asking questions with open-ended responses is not only helpful in removing any last vestiges of misunderstanding but also provides more clarity. Ask questions if you feel as though you haven't fully understood what the other person is saying or if you desire additional clarity on something. It is entirely normal and acceptable to behave in this manner. To avoid interrupting the other person while they are speaking, wait until they have finished before you start asking questions. Do not cut them off in the middle of a statement. Always remember to wait until the appropriate time to ask your question.

You can also show that you are interested in the topic by asking questions that allow for free-form responses. The person who is speaking will have the opportunity to elaborate further on what they have stated as a result of these questions. In addition, it demonstrates that you were attentively listening to whatever it was that they said up until this point. It contributes to the formation of a stronger and more favorable connection between you and the speaker.

No Evaluations

Make sure you don't pass judgment on the person you're listening to if you want to develop your skills as an active listener. It is essential for you to maintain an open mind and pay attention to what they have to say. It makes no difference if you agree with them or disagree with them. Keep in mind that your job right now is to act as an attentive listener, even if you strongly disagree with what they are saying. Nobody inquired about your perspectives and ideas in any way. Do not provide unsolicited counsel; rather, wait to be asked for it before doing so. If you have any questions, you are more than welcome to ask them, and we will be happy to elaborate on what has been stated. However, remember to have an open mind to everything that was discussed. You should go into every conversation with an open mind and make an effort to understand the perspective of the person you are talking to.

To summarize

Let's briefly review some of the most important topics that were covered in this chapter:

You will need to work on becoming a better listener if you want to increase your ability to communicate with others.

Active listening and passive listening are the two categories that fall under the category of listening.

When a person does not actively participate in a conversation and takes in only a portion of the information that is being conveyed to them, they are said to be listening passively.

The following are examples of common obstacles that keep us from listening: being preoccupied with something else, making a conscious decision not to listen, harboring biases that prohibit us from listening to others, and so on.

When a person totally commits themselves to the discourse at hand and makes it a point to ensure that they are taking in all of the information that is being conveyed to them, they are engaging in the practice of active listening.

It will help you recall information better, it will help you prevent misunderstandings, and it will help you create trust with other people. These are the benefits of active listening.

To become a better listener, you need to be able to do the following: rid your mind of any preconceived notions or prejudices, give the other person your undivided attention, read cues from their body language, and check that you have received the information that is being sent to you.

The Four Attributes Necessary for Successful Communication

In order to make up for your lack of communication skills, you need to educate yourself on the four fundamental characteristics of effective communication. These four characteristics are necessary for effective communication with each person and in any setting. They will be elaborated upon throughout the entirety of this book as we explore the various scenarios in which you should communicate in an effective manner.

Choice of Words

It should come as no surprise that the selection of words that you use has a significant bearing on the efficiency with which you interact with other people. When you are unsure about the words to use to convey your meaning, it is easy for that message to be misunderstood when you are communicating with others. It is of the utmost importance that you select the appropriate words to articulate your ideas in a manner that can be comprehended by others.

There are many different approaches you may take to enhance the word choice in your messages. Increasing the size of your vocabulary is one of the most effective things you can do to improve your communication abilities. This is a pretty simple and straightforward task to carry out. You need just add one word per day to your existing vocabulary. You can quickly increase the size of your vocabulary by using one of the many helpful calendars or websites that provide a "word of the day" feature. In spite of the fact that you are already familiar with the word of the day, it is possible that you will learn additional meanings that will enable you to use the term in a more efficient manner.

Generational differences are something that should always be kept in mind when choosing words to use in any kind of communication. From one generation to the next, slang undergoes various shifts. If you are from Generation X and try to speak slang with a Millennial, there is a good chance that you won't be understood. Millennials are members of the generation born between 1980 and

2000. If you are uncertain as to whether another person will understand the slang you are accustomed to using, the safest course of action is to refrain from using it completely.

Idioms and metaphors share the same characteristics. If you want to be understood, you need to select words that are going to be simple for the other person to comprehend. For instance, a person of the younger generation may not know the meaning of the phrase "don't throw the baby out with the bathwater." A person of the older generation is not going to comprehend the phrase "I'm going to go Post Malone on this."

In your communications, it is best not to make the attempt to use the slang of a previous generation. This is another wonderful concept. Even if you are familiar with Millennial slang, it's possible that you don't really understand how it's employed in regular conversation. Because the message will be completely lost, using slang in an inappropriate manner is even worse than using slang in a context in which it is not relatable.

Tone

Your emotions are conveyed to other people through the tone of your voice, which can sometimes make it difficult for them to understand what it is that you are trying to express. Quite sometimes, the meaning of the words we are trying to convey has little to do with the emotions that we are experiencing. When you communicate with other people, your feelings can come out as hostile or annoyed, especially if you are in a foul mood in general or are frustrated with another person or situation.

When this occurs, the meaning of what we say can be misunderstood. For instance, you may be upset about something that occurred at home that morning, and the manner in which you communicate with a subordinate may lead them to believe that you are unhappy with the work that they have done, even when you are stating the exact opposite.

The entirety of our actions, including our vocal inflection, contributes in some way to the communication that we have with other people. It is essential that you keep an even tone that does not get in the way of you communicating what you really mean to the other person. Altering the tone of your voice can also serve to express meaning beyond what you actually say, which is particularly useful if, for instance, you are truly unhappy with the work that someone has done.

The single most helpful thing you can do in any circumstance is to just be mindful of the tone you are employing in your communication. During the course of the conversation, you should consider adjusting your tone of voice if you become aware that you are speaking in a solemn manner when it is not required or when it has the potential to obscure the meaning of what you are saying.

It is also a good idea to avoid bringing any emotions into the conversation at all costs in order to prevent employing the incorrect tone. In order to handle challenging conversations more effectively, cultivate the habit of putting your feelings on pause purposefully. You can help yourself establish the habit of maintaining an even tone regardless of the circumstances by being cognizant of your tone even in instances where it is not as crucial.

Before engaging in discussion, it might be helpful to clear your mind by engaging in some mindful practices like deep breathing and visualizing a positive outcome. For instance, if you had a difficult morning before you arrived at work, and it had the effect of making you upset or furious, you will want to put those feelings to the side before attempting any conversation with your coworkers, bosses, or customers.

It is really not that difficult to carry out at all. The only thing you need to do is close your eyes and remain still for a few minutes. The inhale should last for the count of 5, the hold should last for the count of 7, and the exhale should last for the count of 10. Repeat this a few times while thinking about your go-to spot for peace and quiet. When you are upset with someone, you can also do this to calm yourself down before interacting with them so that your meaning is not obscured by your wrath.

Language of the Body

Again, the way you conduct yourself in general has a significant bearing on how well you are able to communicate with other people. This includes how you carry yourself physically. Your capacity to communicate successfully can be negatively impacted by a variety of bodily motions, including how you hold your body, your posture, what you do with your arms, "talking with your hands," and other movements.

For instance, a lot of people have no idea what to do with their arms when they are standing and having a conversation with someone else. It's not always comfortable to just let your arms hang at your sides like that. Some people find that crossing their arms over their body is the best way to respond to this question.

This action may give the impression to the other person that you are not receptive to what they have to say and are closed off to hearing what they have to say. It is also possible to communicate that you are upset, frustrated, or angry with this expression. Even if none of this is true, the way in which you carry yourself conveys an entirely other message. It is imperative that you never have your arms crossed while participating in conversations, unless you are specifically intending to send a message along these lines.

On the other hand, if you stand with your arms by your sides or clasp your hands behind your back, you are sending a message that you are open to communication. It inspires the other person to engage in conversation on the topic by asking questions and sharing their thoughts. This is a significantly superior exercise that can be used as an alternative to merely letting your arms hang by your sides.

"Talking with your hands" is another habit that can hinder from efficient communication and should be avoided wherever possible. Some individuals move their hands quite a bit when they are speaking, either because they are really enthusiastic about the topic they are discussing or simply because they are at a loss as to what else they could be doing with their hands. All of this additional motion can be highly distracting to the person you are trying to communicate with, and it can take away from the message that you are attempting to send to that person.

Stand with your hands clasped behind your back or in front of you as a good practice. This can also be done in the same way as described earlier. It is impossible for your hands to be in motion while you are speaking if they are clasped together like that. At first, doing so may make you uncomfortable, and you may discover that you are concentrating so intently on suppressing the want to use your hands to communicate that you are unable to keep up with the flow of the conversation. Just bring yourself back to the present when that happens. You will eventually grow used to standing in this manner, and you will become accustomed to not using your hands when you are interacting with other people.

Participatory listening

When trying to convey their ideas to other people, a lot of people make the error of concentrating entirely on the way they communicate with those around them. Saying what you need to communicate in a way that other people can comprehend is only part of what constitutes effective communication. It is also about comprehending what the other person or persons have to say in response and ensuring that you are understood by them.

It is not enough to simply be receptive to what other people have to say in order to engage in active listening. You need to make sure that you are actively listening so that you can understand what is being said. This can be accomplished in a few different ways. Repeating or paraphrasing what the other person has said is the most popular and straightforward approach to practice active listening. For instance, if someone asks you a question, you should restate it and ask them to repeat it so that you may check that you have understood it correctly before you respond.

Putting your active listening skills to practice on a regular basis is the most effective approach to improve them. Employing your active listening abilities is important even when you are having a casual conversation with a stranger. To demonstrate that you have comprehended what they have said, either restate it or paraphrase it. Having conversations with telemarketers is a fantastic method to hone your active listening abilities. Make use of these interactions as a chance to practice active listening rather than immediately hanging up.

You will notice a significant improvement in the efficacy of your interactions with people after you master the ability of active listening. If you are unable to actively listen and gauge whether or not your message is being received, you will be unable to guarantee that your point will be effectively communicated. If you deliberately listen to the other person and find that your message is not being conveyed adequately to them, you have the option of modifying your strategy and attempting to explain yourself in a different way.

Going Forward with It

Following our discussion of the four characteristics of effective communication, the remainder of this book will be devoted to demonstrating how you can apply these characteristics to communication in a variety of settings, such as interpersonal interactions, interactions in the workplace, and social encounters with strangers. You can get a head start on improving your communication abilities by doing the activities described in this chapter, and then you can go on improving your abilities by making use of the exercises described in the next chapters of this book.

Recognizing The Steps In A Productive Communication Cycle

A cycle of effective communication is now something we can relate to.

We talk to one another 24 hours a day, seven days a week, and for the vast majority of our waking hours. It is something that is fundamental to who we are. It would be amazing, wouldn't it, if this important part of ourselves could be moulded, forged, and fine-tuned such that it better serves our interests!

Let's break the cycle down into its component parts as simply as possible.

The individual who initially communicates the message is known as the message's sender. It is the obligation of the sender to encode the message in a way that is both clear and concise. It is absolutely necessary for the sender to comprehend the following in order for there to be efficient communication: • The intended receivers of the message, also known as the target audience

• Furthermore, the reason for sending the message

The sender has some information or knowledge that they want the receiver to have, and they convey it to them in the form of a message. The sender has the option of selecting any mode of communication - verbal, non-verbal, or written - that best serves the goal of their message. This is further personalized based on the manner in which the sender communicates, including their choice of words, actions, and time, as well as their presentation and tone.

In order for there to be effective communication, the message needs to be: • Clearly worded according to the comprehension of the receiver or target audience • Encoded correctly for Call to action, if there is one

Transmission and Noise: When we talk about "transmitting" a message, we're referring to the process of actually sending it. This could be accomplished through a variety of methods of verbal and textual communication. For instance, e-mail, letters, texts, in-person meetings, telephone calls, and video conferences are all forms of communication.

The term "noise" refers to the collection of all of the different elements that have the potential to obstruct the transmission of the sender's message. In addition, this noise might obscure the message, which increases the likelihood that the intended receivers will misunderstand it or that it will not produce the anticipated outcome.

The challenge at hand may pertain to language, where jargon, accent, or language itself is the roadblock to being understood. The noise may be physical, such as when the phone line is not clear or when internet connectivity for video conferencing is poor; the noise may be psychological, such as when the audience is biased or judgmental or when they have assumptions while receiving the message; or the noise may be semantic, which means that the problem lies in the fact that language itself is the roadblock to being understood.

The sender is responsible for ensuring that the message is legible and free of background noise in order for there to be successful communication. encode the message in such a way that it takes into account the possibility of noise eruption.

There are no issues with the transmission or the channels through which it is sent; Conduct some tests on the channels before it is necessary for any critical communication to take place.

Receiver: Simply said, the receiver is the person who obtains the message and then understands it by decoding its many components, which may include text, pictures, audios, visual props, and so on. If the recipient understands both the meaning and the context of the message in the same way that the sender intended it to be understood, then we can confidently conclude that effective communication has taken place.

In this scenario, for there to be effective communication, the receiver needs to ensure the following things in order for the information to be received correctly: That the channels of receiving are clean and free of noise; That there are no biases and preconceptions that color the message that was meant.

Cooperate with the sender to ensure that your response includes unmistakable indications of understanding.

Feedback is the single most important component of every communication system. This indicates to the sender that the message was received and comprehended without any ambiguity or room for misinterpretation on the part of the recipient.

In order to ensure that there is effective communication:

The audience's response, whether vocal or non-verbal, must be gathered in a timely manner and can take either form.

The message needs to be modified in accordance with the feedback.

Employing public relations experts?

There is a possibility that public relations firms of varying hues and sizes will continue to pitch their services to your organization in the hopes of being given the opportunity to interact with your communication strategy and execution. And we have always noticed that companies are only looking for these things: does your agency have the scale, size, and a national or international presence, and would you be able to reach across all (including social) media, in every nook and cranny of the planet!

There is nothing wrong with doing this, and in fact, it is very vital to check on the credentials that your potential agency already possesses! However, at the same time, it is essential to keep in mind that the PR agency you hire must have the capacity as well as the flexibility to engage in the public relations strategy and implementation of an organization like yours.

You could hire the very best agency in the known universe, but before you do so, consider the following: is there a point in doing so if their strengths do not sync with the scale and strength of your company? What if their capabilities are more specific to large sized companies, and not for the kind of company that yours is – a niche small organization, but with its own unique service offerings or qualities?

When you feel that it is time to hire a PR agency, why don't you check for the following few things first? Does the firm have a track record of providing PR value to businesses that are comparable to yours, and if so, how frequently have they done so?

Do they have the flexibility, not only in their own pitch, but also in how they appear to fit into your scheme of things? Would they find synergy in working with a client who is similar to this?

Do they have the kind of dedication to work with companies like you over the medium and long terms, such that you finally reap the actual benefit of interacting with an agency? if they do, then you should ask this question. Alternately, if you are only interested in receiving sporadic amounts of media coverage, there is no need to invest time in conducting an in-depth investigation of the agency.

Do they possess the de-learning skills necessary to adjust to your specific requirements? This is of the utmost significance. Large and multinational agencies, whether you like it or not, come with a mindset, and even if they are willing to do their best, they may not be able to if your communication demands are radically different from their own.

Do they have an awareness of the specific needs that your sector has, and are they prepared to devote the time and effort necessary to get insights into how your media visibility compares to that of your competitors?

Are they just another agency that churns out generic press releases? Or do they conduct in-depth research on you, determine what aspects of your life are most successful, and highlight those aspects?

How much more credibility and improved image value can they bring to the table (not just across, but over the course of about two to three months)?

Do they fit into the modern era? Do they have a social life in the conventional sense? Do they, in a practical sense, make it easier for journalists to report on a variety of contemporary topics relevant to the beat or industry that they cover?

If your requirements are more regional, do they have any insight into what is successful in the market or geography where you are located?

It is possible that a public relations strategy that is simple to implement in one region or part of the world is not feasible in another region or part of the world due to differences in the required skill sets or delivery capabilities.

When it comes to the management of your organization's reputation, you may find that there are a great many factors that need to be taken into consideration before you request proposals from public relations firms.

Consciousness Of Oneself

It is crucial that you learn how to adjust your thinking to become more self-aware before we get into the tactics that can help you become more assertive. In other words, you need to understand how to become more self-aware before we can even begin to discuss the techniques. The way in which you perceive yourself is an essential component in determining how you interact with other people.

Let's pretend we've traveled back in time to the year 1100 CE. We are currently making a list of characteristics that we feel to be admirable in a family member, coworker, lover, or friend. We are seated on a wooden bench while holding a quill. Which of those qualities should we put on this quaint little list? What are some of the possibilities? It's possible that traits like patience, charity, loyalty, and kindness are what it takes. Now, let's bring things back up to the present day. Even though we are sitting in a contemporary living room and writing up a comparable list on our computer or phone, there is a strong probability that we will scribble down the same virtues as we did back in the year 1100, but some fresh ideas might get added. In point of fact, I'd add self-awareness as a positive quality in a person to the list. But what exactly is meant by the term "self-awareness"?

Understanding oneself entails being able to identify and control one's feelings. The origins of this word can be traced back to Carl Jung and Sigmund Freud. However, the book Emotional

Intelligence by Daniel Goleman, which was published in 1995, is likely where our current idea of self-awareness originated. To put it another way, self-awareness refers to a person's capacity to accurately detect their own mental state at any given moment. The majority of us aren't even conscious of how we're feeling most of the time, and that's the problem. In addition, we are not aware of the extent to which our feelings shape our thoughts and actions. When we have a better handle on our emotional states, we will have an easier time managing other elements of our lives.

Self-awareness also gives you the ability to step outside of yourself and observe how the actions and words you choose influence other people. It's a form of introspection that doesn't isolate you from the outside world, but rather invites the outside world inside so you can evaluate how it ties in with how you feel and how you behave.

The vast majority of us are under the false impression that we are self-aware, when in reality, we are not. People have a tendency to have a skewed perception of how self-aware they really are. They have a false sense of self-awareness, as they do not know themselves as well as they believe. They may have even avoided increasing self-awareness because doing so required an honest examination of themselves, which can bring about a great deal of uncomfortable sensations that need to be dealt with.

In any event, having a genuine sense of self-awareness is extremely beneficial. A lack of self-awareness used to be dismissed as a harmless human quirk; however, as our world continues to evolve, the necessity of cultivating self-awareness has taken on a larger level of significance. If you are able to keep control of your own feelings, you will be in a better position to influence the feelings of other people, whether they are members of your family, people you encounter in social settings, or coworkers and customers at your place of employment.

Boost Your Own Self-Confidence

When you have self-confidence, you have faith in your own capabilities as well as your own opinions. Despite any flaws you may possess or the opinions of others, you still hold a high regard for yourself and believe that you are deserving of respect.

The terms "self-esteem" and "self-efficacy" are frequently interchanged with "self-confidence," despite the fact that these concepts are somewhat distinct from one another. When we realize that we have accomplished a goal or become proficient in a skill, we experience a feeling of self-efficacy. Because of this, we are better able to believe that if we put in a lot of effort and continue to educate ourselves in a specific field, we will be successful. Having this level of self-assurance enables you to take on difficult projects and remain resolute in the face of failure.

Self-esteem can be defined as the conviction that the people around you like and approve of you. You might or might not have the power to regulate these feelings, and if you receive rejection or criticism from other people, it could have a negative impact on your self-esteem if you don't find strategies to maintain it.

When it comes to being forceful, confidence is a crucial component to have. If you lack self-assurance, you will be less likely to advocate for yourself in social situations. Simply put, you do not believe that you are deserving of having your wants met or your thoughts voiced.

Let's have a look at how you can determine whether or not you have self-assurance. The following instances illustrate the distinction between behaviors that are regarded as exhibits of confidence and behaviors that reveal a lack of self-confidence in the individual.

Actions Taken With Confidence

Kindly accept praises by saying, "Thank you, I worked really hard on that." I'm happy that you can see how much effort I put into it.

anticipating praise and admiration for your many successes.

recognizing that you were wrong and gaining wisdom as a result of your actions.

willing to take a chance and go the extra mile in order to provide a superior product.

Do what you believe to be right even though it may lead to criticism or ridicule from others.

Behaviors Associated with Low Self-Confidence

Refuting the compliments given, he said, "That project wasn't anything. Anyone may have carried out the deed.

Apologizing to other people for your own shortcomings.

Attempting to hide the errors you've made or maintaining the hope that you'll be able to correct them before anyone else finds out about them.

The practice of remaining within one's comfort zone, avoiding taking risks, and being petrified of making a mistake.

determining your behavior based on the opinions of other people.

People who are comfortable in their own skin tend to have a more optimistic outlook. They place a high value on themselves, and they have faith in their own judgment. The upbeat news is that you can improve your self-assurance with practice. The following are some ways that you can exude confidence:

Communication via Body Language

You need to assume a more open posture if you want to look and feel more confident. This will help. Maintain a straight stance or posture while sitting. You should either keep your hands folded in your lap or rest them on the sides of your body. It is inappropriate to stand with your hands on your hips. This demonstrates that you want to take control of the situation. Never ever slump over!

Always remember to keep a level mind. You shouldn't lean either backward or forward. When giving a presentation, it's important to use motions with open hands. Spread your hand out in front of you and maintain the palm facing the audience when you want to "point" to something. This demonstrates that you are open to exchanging thoughts and communicating with others. Make sure that your upper arms are kept in a close position to your torso.

Engage in Direct Dialogue with One Another.

Every element of your existence requires that you interact with other people. Make and maintain eye contact with the other person while you are interacting with them in any way. It demonstrates that you are interested in what they have to say when you do something like this. In addition to this, it demonstrates that you are an engaged participant in the discussion. Keep in mind that people of different cultures use their bodies in very different ways. In your region of the world, some hand gestures may have one meaning, but in other parts of the world they may have an entirely other significance. As a consequence of this, it is very feasible to insult another person without ever having to utter a word and despite the fact that you harbor no ill intent against that person. If you are going to give a presentation or are going to be dealing with folks from different countries, do some research.

During a conversation, you should never divert your gaze from the other person or fidget with your hands. It's possible that this will make you appear worried or inattentive. Make sure that your handshake is solid whenever you shake hands with someone at work, as this may be the standard greeting. You don't want it to be overly strict, and you definitely don't want to go crazy if you don't know the individual very well. It is possible that the other person will interpret your attempt to grab hold of their shoulder or wrist with your other hand as a display of power. Therefore, you shouldn't do this the first time you meet someone new because it's not a good idea. Try not to make the interaction uncomfortable or unpleasant in any way.

AN APPROPRIATE USE OF BODY LANGUAGE

You may improve your chances of success in the job by making strategic use of body language in a number of different ways. The reactions of those around you might be influenced by your body language. In the same vein, it can impact how others see you and how their expectations of you change. Your productivity and reputation on the job might be affected by how well you are aware of and pay attention to your own body language. It's possible that a group's use of body language can help them become more authentic, more willing to compromise, and better at working together. You can demonstrate to your manager and your coworkers that you are valuable to the company by developing your ability to read and interpret body language.

INSTRUCTIONS IN A STEP-BY-STEP PROCESS FOR COMPREHENDING BODY LANGUAGE

In order to increase both your comprehension of and ability to use body language, there are a few steps you may take. These means include things like:

Consider your surroundings carefully.

Demonstrate compassion.

Be naturally mindful in your actions.

AFFECTIVE PERCEPTION

To begin correcting problematic body language, the first step is to observe it. It's possible that developing your perceptual abilities won't be as difficult of a task as you would think it will be. It's likely that from this point forward, you'll be constantly interpreting body language without even realizing it. Take into consideration the representative in your place of employment who is the friendliest to you. Do they smile at you when you walk past them in the lobby? When you talk to them, do they gesture and maintain in touch with you physically? It's likely that the way they carry themselves contributes to your impression that they are friendly.

You will need to widen the scope of your attention if you want to get better at interpreting body language. In terms of body language, mindfulness refers to the practice of making a concerted effort to pay attention to the actions of other people and to the world around you. If you put your attention on learning the regular behavioral norms of other people, you will give yourself a better chance of successfully decoding the nonverbal correspondence they provide you. Anxiety and unease frequently manifest itself in the form of ricocheting or shaking one's leg under the table. On the other hand, if you notice that your boss always seems to shake their leg when they are excited or interested, you will have the opportunity to correctly interpret their body language when they are in such states.

DISPLAY SOME COMPASSION

This trend connects back to our earlier conversation about taking into account body language within the context of its appropriate use. It's possible that the best way to understand the body language of another person is to put yourself in their shoes and see the world from their perspective. You can improve your ability to decipher what someone else's body language may be saying by considering factors such as their personality or the particular nuances of their situation. For instance, if you meet a colleague and he avoids making eye contact, purses his lips, and folds his arms, you might conclude that he is upset with you or that he is disappointed in you. However, if he is anxious to identify himself, he may realize that he is under a lot of strain owing to a closing time that is approaching soon. You are able to acquire a more comprehensive knowledge of their body language and the meaning it conveys if you think about their conditions.

BE NATURALLY AND MINDFULLY PRESENT

Becoming more aware of the nonverbal cues you send out to others is the third stage toward enhancing your relationship body language skills. If you are an expert in analyzing the body language of others, but you are unaware of your own, it is possible that you are not communicating to the best of your ability. Being naturally aware of your body language entails watching how you actually interact with other people, taking command of your external appearances, and moving in a way that has a certain intention behind it. You can improve the ability to demonstrate interest, dedication, and proven expertise by using body language if you practice your non-verbal correspondence regularly and give yourself plenty of opportunities to do so.

On-the-job communication relies heavily on nonverbal cues, particularly body language. Your capacity for reading, comprehending, and interpreting body language will expand in direct proportion to the degree to which you develop these skills. You can enhance your effect and efficiency in the workplace by improving your use of nonverbal correspondence. You can do this by improving your use of this guide as well as other resources. The acquisition of skills in body language can be a valuable resource for you on your journey toward becoming a successful and important communicator.

Learning to read and respond appropriately with your body language is a skill that may be quite useful throughout your career. However, it also has the potential to be a setback. We are able to measure language at much slower rates than the speeds at which we measure physiological signals. Therefore, exercise caution in the way that you put yours to use!

Communication And Models - Models Are Helpful In Communicating Since They Assist You Communicate

Although there are various perspectives from which to examine communications, being familiar with the models presented here can benefit you in ways that you may not have anticipated. It goes without saying that modeling may be used in a wide variety of contexts, and I have no doubt that you make use of this kind of strategy in your day-to-day job.

Any writer who has written about Leonardo DiCaprio will be able to tell you that models are, of course, just a small part of the narrative. This part is included before the "how to" section because you need to have some comprehension of these concepts in order to use them when developing your communications strategy and tactics in the next section.

Because there are many other communication models floating about in the media industry, and many more than I could or would even want to get into here, I will limit myself to a handful of the more traditional ones. It is important for you to understand that the world is a large place, and that your message is just a little part of the media environment that is contending for attention; hence, making use of an established communication model is a smart place to begin.

Because the aforementioned examples are only scraping the surface, it is my hope that this brief and succinct introduction to the various communication models will give you some indication of how much more material is available. The purpose of this article is to provide you with a concise overview of many of the various communication models that are now available.

The hypodermic model, also known as the syringe hypothesis, is the one communication model that I see most often in #SciComm. It is also one that you should be familiar with since it is essentially what you see in a lot of different forms of mass media. The public's mind is being artificially implanted with media content literally on a daily basis.

In the case of a movie or a documentary, the creators first craft the message, and then they release it into the world in the hopes that it will be seen and appreciated. As soon as it is available to the public, the task at hand is finished. The idea could not be more straightforward; yet, it is not the only one, and this model is devoid of any sophistication. It is the communications version of shouting into a megaphone while standing on a busy intersection.

The linear model is the next level in communications models, and here is the point when it begins to have a great deal of importance to you personally.

The linear Sender-Message-Channel-Receiver model was discovered by Berlo, and I strongly urge that you understand this one as it is an extension on the Hypodermic Model and offers a lot more flavor; it forces you to think a lot more about the message you are generating and how you want it to be received. In other words, I truly suggest that you grasp this one because it is an expansion on the Hypodermic Model and adds a lot more flavor.

Therefore, it is clear from this that, in contrast to the Hypodermic model, in which the sender simply injects the message into the receiver, Berlo is arguing that you should take into account your abilities, knowledge, social system, and culture; you should also dissect the message in terms of its structure and codes; and you should think about the channel through which you will be transmitting the message.

These channels do not only refer to the five literal senses; rather, in this context, you need to take into consideration, for instance, the unspoken words that send a message that we all comprehend as well as the non-verbal communications that we perceive such as body language as well as the symbols that we grasp without an explanation. Because there is more to communication than the words that are spoken, this should serve as a reminder to evaluate the less evident aspects of the message in addition to the words that are sent. It comes down to how well you and the models can collaborate to produce a message via the process of working together.

In the world of music, there is a proverb that goes something like this: "It's not the notes you play; it's the notes you don't play." That is the portion of the message that is not stated explicitly but is understood by most people (eye roll). It's true that content is king, but subtext is where it's at.

And then, as a last step, you have thought about the manner in which the audience absorbs the message. Do they possess the same levels of knowledge and expertise as you, as well as the similar cultural background? In such case, you will need to adjust the content of your message. The unfortunate reality is that Google Translate is not an option for this, therefore you will need to perform some independent research.

Here is when the message's underlying semiotics start to become relevant to the conversation. What do the symbols and codes signify to you, and more importantly, what do they imply to the people who are listening to you? For some people, seeing an image of a dinosaur denotes that the narrative is about dinosaurs and that the individual enjoys learning about them, but for others, it indicates that the individual is questioning the fundamental foundation of their religious beliefs.

After all, evolution is nothing more than a hypothesis, right?

It is not always possible to translate the symbols and codes of one culture into those of another culture, and a theory is the best illustration of this phenomenon. The horse has fled when it comes to that signifier, and there is nothing you can do to reverse it; all you can do is attempt to describe it in a new manner. But Berlo's approach will assist you in explaining it in a new manner, by having you consider the receiver of the message before you produce it. This is an important step in the process.

The linear model developed by Berlo is distinct from the hypodermic model in that, in the linear model, consideration is given to the audience that will be receiving the message and how they will understand it. While the hypodermic model is used to transmit film, there is not much room for adaptation when it comes to the audience. On the other hand, this model is not used in the promotion of the picture. In this part of the process, they take into account the audience and adjust the messaging to assist sell the product. When a film is released in many areas, the trailers, posters, and merchandise for each region will often be unique.

I produced a case study on the marketing strategy that was employed for Rogue One: A Star Wars Story, looking at the marketplaces in both the United States and China. Because there is no comparable cultural past associated with Star Wars in China as there is in the West, the marketing strategy has to be modified to take this into consideration.

Then of course for social media, they again utilize a different model, and the next one I'll be talking about, as you may have noticed there is something lacking from Berlo's approach, and that something is feedback from the audience.

Feedback is beneficial, because it enables one to become a better communicator (as well as a guitarist) when it is handled in an efficient manner. But for the time being, let's take a look at feedback in the context of various communication models. I'll be discussing about feedback later on.

Although the absence of feedback is a fault, it is not one that prevents the model developed by Berlo from being a useful instrument for you to use. Let's take a look at Schramm's model of communication for the time being since we need to look at a model that does incorporate it right now.

Therefore, what does this imply?

The person sending the message is represented by the encoder on the left, while the person receiving the message is represented by the decoder on the right. The communication is received, interpreted, and then feedback is encoded into a message that is sent back to the person who sent the message in the first place.

Remember that the interpretation process can be seen in the Berlo model, and that it is the communication skills, attitude, knowledge, social system, and culture that translate the message into something that can be understood by the receiver and transmitted back to the sender, thereby creating a loop of communication. This is something that is important to keep in mind here.

This concept is readily seen as a conversation between two individuals, in which each participant is picking up on not just the verbal and nonverbal communication, but also all of the other components at the same time, and altering their message as they go along depending on the feedback received from the other participant in the discussion.

Schramm's approach also illustrates something really fundamental about communication, and I'm trying to incorporate as much of it as I can in this book as a result of the fact that it's such an important topic. It has to do with the kind of work that you perform.

Schramm was implying that in order to fit the requirements of this field of experience, a message must be encoded, and this may be expressed in a few different straightforward ways. What is the best way to describe an airplane to someone who has never been on one?

They have no idea that heavier-than-air flying is even theoretically feasible, much alone that it is possible for humans to round the globe in one. It is more likely that, in order to explain it, you will need to describe it as a giant bird that was constructed by humans and that people can fly inside it, rather than on. This is what is meant by the term "field of experience."

You are encoding the message so that it may be understood by the receiver based on their cultural knowledge and the experiences they have had.

According to Schramm, effective communication requires that the sender have a grasp of the recipient's sphere of experience in connection to their own. It's possible that some people may accuse this of watering down science, but if they do, it only shows how narrow their own experience is. They are unable of comprehending the fact that not everyone can reap the advantages of their knowledge.

When we consider both Berlo's and Schramm's models together, we find that they seem to be something that everyone of us can contribute to. However, there is still another significant communication model known as the Interactive or Convergence model, and noise is a part of this particular model.

This model is composed of two different linear models, similar to Berlo's, except they are stacked on top of one another and move in the opposite direction.

In this case, the response isn't instantaneous but rather spread out over a longer period of time. You might think of it as publishing something on social media, waiting to see how your audience responds to it, and then modifying your next message to take into mind the response you received from them.

However, what about the noise that I described? Now that we've got that out of the way, let's talk about everything else that might prevent the audience from seeing, hearing, and understanding your message. This might be anything, from the sheer amount of postings on social media to the person sitting next to them carrying on a conversation to the person sitting next to them thinking about their day, etc.

If you want to be an effective communicator in today's society, you simply can't afford to ignore the noise around you. Because there is so much of it in our society, which is saturated with media, and because we all have so little time that is actually ours to spare, you are in competition with everyone on the globe to get your message out.

And if you're asking which of these models is the best one for #SciComm, the answer is that it really depends on the platform or channel you're using, what you're trying to say, and most crucially, how you're choosing to say it. If you're wondering which model is best, the answer is that it truly depends.

When you are considering how you will develop your message, you will discover that you will be employing Berlo's model quite a bit, along with Schramm's fields of experience for good measure. This is something that you can expect to happen. It wasn't simple for me to decide which models to discuss here since I didn't want to overwhelm you with too many information.

When it comes to them, it is much too simple to lose sight of the forest for the trees, yet having even a fundamental grasp of them will be beneficial to you. If the only thing you get out of this book is the idea that you should consider your audience before composing any message, then I would consider myself a very successful author.

Pick Your Partner From The Box

Supplies required for this activity are blank pieces of paper, pencils, and markers.

The bare minimum required is between 20 and 25 persons.

Time: around forty-five minutes

Drawing is one way that a child or teenager with Asperger syndrome (AS) may cultivate new ideas and give vent to his or her creativity, which was the motivation for the invention of this activity.

The leader of the group will split everyone up into pairs, give each of them a piece of paper, some pencils, and some markers, and then explain them on how to play the game, telling each player that he or she has to sketch his or her partner. In order to do this assignment successfully, he or she will need to take into consideration both their qualities and their interests.

For instance, the child or adolescent with AS will visualize whether his partner is tall or short, fat or skinny, detail his features, and take into account his interests. This means that he can draw him as he is, and also if his partner likes to read, sing, dance, or play, he will try to draw him engaging in one of those activities or with some of his most prized objects of entertainment to the side.

At the conclusion, they will each present the other their designs and will have the opportunity to add additional components based on the suggestions made by their peers.

Because of this exercise, children and adolescents with AS will have the ability to recognize that things often go beyond what is presented on the surface, and that if they think about them carefully, they can construct things and make them more enjoyable to play with. This will excite their imaginations and encourage them to develop new things.

www.ingramcontent.com/pod-product-compliance
Lightning Source LLC
Chambersburg PA
CBHW050242120526
44590CB00016B/2188